fimbles™

Activity Book

Meet the Fimbles

Colour in the pictures of Fimbo, Florrie and Baby Pom. Join the dots to write the Fimbles' names.

Hello. I'm Fimbo.

Fimbo

Hello. I'm Florrie.

Florrie

Hello. I'm Baby Pom.

Pom

Spot the Difference

Can you spot 5 differences between the 2 pictures?

Special Things

Match the Fimbles to their special things.

Shimmy Shaker

Little One

Trundle Truck

Fimbo

Baby Pom

Florrie

Draw Rockit

Copy the picture of Rockit onto the grid opposite, then colour him in.

Maze

Help the Fimbles find the apple and
the cracker hidden in the maze.

Picnic Time!

The Fimbles and their friends are having a picnic.
Draw different foods on the plate for them to eat.

Matching Pairs

Match up the tops and bottoms of the Fimbles and their friends, by drawing a line between them.

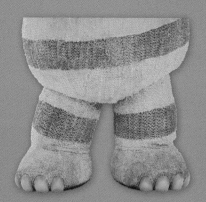

Roly Mo's Story

Who is Roly Mo
reading a story to?

Dot-to-Dot

Who am I? Join the dots and colour me in.

Baby Pom

Help Baby Pom find her way across the
Purple Meadow towards the Tinkling Tree.
Follow the path.

Hidden Crackers

Find the crackers hidden in this picture. How many are there?

Who's Who?

Match the Fimbles to their silhouettes, by drawing a line.

Counting

How many Shimmy Shakers, Little Ones and Trundle Trucks are there?

Answers: 5 Shimmy Shakers, 3 Little Ones and 1 Trundle Truck.

Fimbo

Finish this picture of Fimbo.

Dot-to-Dot

Join the dots to find out who this is, then colour the picture in.

Double Puzzle

There are 2 exciting puzzles for you to do. Cut out the pieces and use the pictures on this page to help you make each puzzle. Once you have completed one puzzle, turn over your puzzle pieces and make the second puzzle.

Odd One Out

Which Bessie is the odd one out?

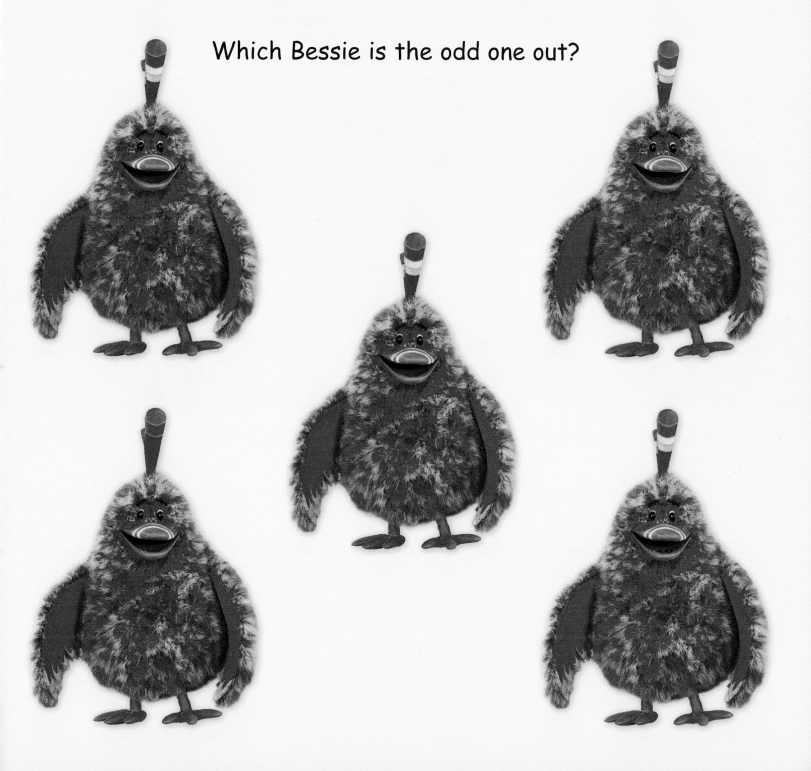

Goodbye!

Come and find us again!

Fimbo

Baby Pom

Colour in the 3 Fimbles.

Florrie